Building Skills in Writing

Report Writing

BY KAREN KELLAHER

SCHOLASTIC
PROFESSIONAL BOOKS

NEW YORK • TORONTO • LONDON • AUCKLAND • SYDNEY
MEXICO CITY • NEW DELHI • HONG KONG • BUENOS AIRES

To my father,
Joseph Burns

Front cover and interior design by Kathy Massaro
Cover art by Jon Buller
Interior art by Michael Moran
Poster art by Laura Cornell

ISBN: 0-439-28842-8
Copyright © 2002 by Karen Kellaher
Published by Scholastic Inc.
All rights reserved.
Printed in the U.S.A.

1 2 3 4 5 6 7 8 9 10   40   09 08 07 06 05 04 03 02

Contents

* INCLUDES REPRODUCIBLE KIDS' PAGE(S)

Introduction

ABOUT THIS SERIES:
Building Skills in Writing

Most of us write every day. We write when we make a grocery list, when we e-mail a faraway friend, and when we prepare our lesson plans. But rarely do we stop to think about what we're really doing when we put pen to paper or fingers to keyboard. What, exactly, is writing?

Educator Donald Murray once said that writing is the act of using language to "discover meaning in experience and communicate it."* For me, this definition sums up the most important aspects of the writing process. First, it reminds us that writing is rooted in personal experience. Without experience, we have no meaning to communicate. Second, Murray's definition underscores the fact that writing always has a purpose and an audience. The very idea of "communicating" meaning implies that there is someone to receive the message, even if that audience is simply oneself at a later moment in time.

As teachers of emergent writers, you have an exciting job—to help bring this definition to life for your students. This series, *Building Skills in Writing*, is designed to assist you in this role. Each of the three books—*Report Writing, Story Writing,* and *Responding to Literature*—features lessons, strategies, activities, reproducibles, teaching tips, rubrics, and checklists to help your students write for a specific purpose and audience. Each addresses all stages of the writing process, from prewriting through publishing and assessment.

ABOUT THIS BOOK:
Report Writing

Not long ago, my grandmother found the first research report I ever wrote—a short report on Hawaii, complete with stick-figure drawings of women in hula skirts. I was in second grade when I received the assignment, and I remember having no idea where to begin. I lived in Pennsylvania, had never traveled to Hawaii, and knew absolutely nothing about the Aloha State. What "saved" me was the *World Book Encyclopedia* set my parents had purchased, one volume at a time, at the supermarket. (It's a good thing I was not asked to write about Nebraska, since we had somehow missed the "N" volume!) Not knowing any better, I enthusiastically copied facts straight from the reference book. Thankfully, I later learned more effective strategies for writing reports.

Don't get me wrong; my first report was not a complete waste of time. I

* *Learning by Teaching: Selected Articles on Writing and Teaching.* Upper Montclair, New Jersey: Boynton/Cook, 1982, p. 10

learned how to find information, how to present a report neatly, and even how to add pictures for visual impact. But when I think about what I'd like today's students to gain from their early research and writing experiences, I hope it will be a great deal more. I'd like them to feel a connection to the topics they write about and to explore various sources of information. I'd like them to put the material in their own words, organize it in a way that makes sense to them, and to feel a sense of ownership and mastery. Chances are, those are the same goals you have for your students. This book can help.

Specifically, the book will help you teach students to:

◎ write to inform, using various report formats.

◎ take effective notes and use graphic organizers.

◎ identify a topic that is interesting and of appropriate scope.

◎ develop a topic with facts, details, examples, and explanations.

◎ exclude extraneous and inappropriate information.

◎ edit for grammar, punctuation, spelling, and capitalization.

◎ evaluate their own and others' reports using checklists.

TEACHING WITH THE POSTER:
Recipe for Good Writing— Red-Hot Reports

Tucked into this book you'll find a full-color poster on the report-writing process. Display the poster in a central location in your classroom and refer to it often as students research and write their reports. If you've got some handy, share samples of well-written student reports from past years. Point out how the writer incorporated the ingredients listed on the poster: topic, research questions, main ideas, supporting details, examples, graphic aids. By following the recipe and throwing in some of their own unique spices, your students will soon be writing research reports that sizzle!

To help students remember the poster's tips, use the Red-Hot Reports reproducible on page 6 to make learning place mats. The reproducible is an exact replica of the poster and is designed for students to color, then tape to their desks or insert in binders for homework help. For best results, laminate the place mats or glue them onto sheets of construction paper.

Correlations With the Language Arts Standards

The activities in this book are aligned with the following language arts standards outlined by the Mid-Continent Regional Educational Laboratory (MCREL), an organization that collects and synthesizes noteworthy national and state K–12 curriculum standards.

◎ Gathers and uses information for research purposes:
  ● uses a variety of strategies to plan research
  ● uses a variety of sources to gather information for research

◎ Writes expository compositions:
  ● identifies and stays on the topic
  ● develops the topic with facts and details
  ● excludes extraneous information
  ● provides a concluding statement
  ● lists resources by title

◎ Uses prewriting strategies such as graphic organizers and note-taking to plan written work

◎ Uses strategies to draft, organize, and revise written work

◎ Uses strategies to edit and publish written work

◎ Evaluates own and others' work

Source: *A Compendium of Standards and Benchmarks for K–12 Education* (Mid-Continent Regional Educational Laboratory, 1995).

6

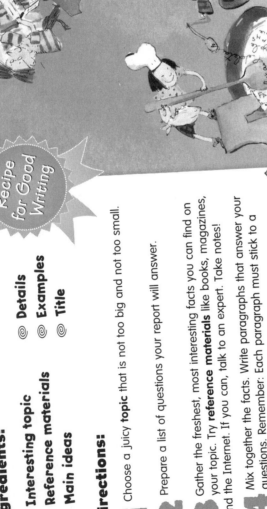

Red-Hot Reports

Recipe for Good Writing

Ingredients:

- ◎ Interesting topic
- ◎ Reference materials
- ◎ Main ideas
- ◎ Details
- ◎ Examples
- ◎ Title

Directions:

1 Choose a juicy **topic** that is not too big and not too small.

2 Prepare a list of questions your report will answer.

3 Gather the freshest, most interesting facts you can find on your topic. Try **reference materials** like books, magazines, and the Internet. If you can, talk to an expert. Take notes!

4 Mix together the facts. Write paragraphs that answer your questions. Remember: Each paragraph must stick to a **main idea**!

5 Add a spoonful of **details** and **examples** to support each main idea.

6 Arrange your sentences and paragraphs in an order that makes sense. Garnish your report with a tangy **title**.

7 Before serving, remove any mistakes in grammar and spelling. Ask a partner to read your report and help you find ways to spice it up.

Serving Suggestion:

Add a pinch of colorful pictures, graphs, or charts to make your report more interesting.

ILLUSTRATION BY LAURA CORNELL

Building Skills in Writing: Report Writing   Scholastic Professional Books

Getting Started: Choosing a Topic

One of the things I love about children is their insatiable curiosity. Several years ago, when I was editing a current-events magazine for third-graders, students would write to me with the most interesting questions:

◎ *Why do some caterpillars become moths and other ones become butterflies?*

◎ *What is the most endangered animal in the world? Why?*

◎ *Were there kids at the first Thanksgiving? What did they do for fun?*

There was no room in the magazine to respond to such queries, but I wrote back to each student, pointing out the incredible resources available at a school or local library. There, I assured each letter writer, he or she would find detailed answers—as well as some interesting new questions.

Ironically, when a teacher announces that it's report-writing time, this natural curiosity sometimes flies right out the window. "I don't know what to write about!" many students complain. Though it may seem that the easiest solution is to simply assign a topic to each child, that leaves students out of an important part of the writing process. When students choose the topic they are to research and report on, they are more actively involved in the learning process—and they tend to develop a sense of ownership that motivates them from prewriting through publishing. Here are some strategies for helping your students choose topics that work for them. The strategies are divided into three categories: Brainstorming Themes, Checking Scope, and Forming Research Questions.

Brainstorming Themes

At this stage, students are simply garnering ideas. They have not yet checked the scope of their topic or developed specific research questions.

BRAINSTORMING STRATEGY 1:
Make It Personal

(Use with Kids' Page 11.)

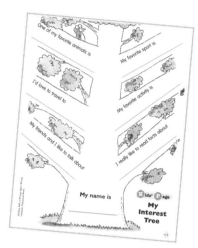

The best topics for research reports are those with which students have had some personal connection or experience. Encourage students to brainstorm topics that relate to their own interests and lives in some way. At the same time, help them avoid topics that they already know so much about, they don't need to do any research!

1 Using the My Interest Tree reproducible on page 11, have students each write down six or more subject areas that hold particular appeal for them. Students can use the prompts on the branches to describe their interests.

2 Help each student narrow his or her topics to one that will translate into an interesting research topic. In some cases you'll need to help children look at a topic a little bit differently. For example, if a student wrote that she likes to read about weather, help her select one aspect, such as blizzards, thunderstorms, or rainbows.

BRAINSTORMING STRATEGY 2:
Connect to Your Curriculum

The wonderful thing about writing is that it can help students learn across the curriculum. To integrate writing into your social studies or science lessons, invite students to brainstorm report topics that connect to what you're studying. You'll be amazed at the variety of topics students tackle. Here are some examples of approaches you might take:

Science: Studying the rain forest? Have students choose one aspect of the forest to write about. For example, they might research an animal or plant native to this habitat, a problem that threatens the rain forest, or the climate conditions there.

Materials

- copy of Kids' Page 11 for each student

STEP 1

Social Studies: While learning about communities, students might write reports on what a mayor does or how your local post office organizes and delivers letters. They could write about how your community got started or compare it with another community elsewhere.

Language Arts: Invite students to choose a favorite author and write a report on his or her life. Some students might prefer to research and write about an art style they admired in a picture book.

You'll notice that in each of the above examples, students still have a great deal of freedom in choosing a topic, although certain parameters have been set.

BRAINSTORMING STRATEGY 3:

Use Field Trips and Special Events

A field trip to an interesting locale or a visit from a special speaker can serve as a springboard for topic selection. Let students know ahead of time that they will be choosing report topics based on the visit or experience. Encourage them to take notes and then hone in on an aspect of the visit or discussion that interested them. Here are some examples:

◎ If the flu and colds are making the rounds at your school, invite a pediatric nurse to speak to the class about good health and nutrition. Invite students to follow up with research reports on germ prevention, the importance of vitamins, or common illnesses—whatever aspect of the discussion piqued their interest.

◎ After a field trip to a natural history museum, one student might report on what an archaeologist does, while another looks at the differences between a Tyrannosaurus Rex and a Brachiosaurus. Still another student might explore theories about what caused dinosaurs to become extinct.

Using field trips and other special events as catalysts for reports gives an authentic context to writing. Students get to research questions they want to know more about, rather than start from scratch with an assigned topic that holds no interest for them.

BRAINSTORMING STRATEGY 4: **Use the Media**

Another way to spark ideas for research reports is to provide plenty of exposure to nonfiction media, especially magazines and newspapers geared to your students' reading level. Because these media offer a broad overview of many topics, your students will be able to pick and choose what catches their interest. See below for a list of recommended periodicals.

1 Set up a media table with more than enough nonfiction periodicals for everyone in the class. Be sure to cover an array of interest areas. Invite each student to select a magazine or newspaper to read.

2 Allow time for students to page through the periodicals and read several of the articles. Have each student choose one topic from the periodical that he or she would like to research further. For example, a student might want to focus on King Tut after reading about Egyptian mummies. What makes this strategy especially kid-friendly is that students have their first source of information right at their fingertips. They can take notes from the article before moving on to other books and resources. (See Chapter 2.)

Selected Periodicals for Second- and Third-Graders

Check ordering information—titles may be subscription-only.

Kids Discover

A fact-filled magazine for children ages 6 to 12. Each issue has a nonfiction theme suitable for student research reports, from DNA to dinosaurs. Call 1-888-779-2574.

National Geographic World

Students can read about geography, wildlife, science, and more. Log on to **www.nationalgeographic.com/world/**

Ranger Rick

A lively nature magazine with articles on such topics as habitats, animal migration, coral reefs, hurricanes, and much more. Log on to **www.nwf.org/kids/**

Scholastic News

Scholastic offers editions of this current-events magazine geared specifically to each grade level. It is designed for classroom use and includes a teacher's edition and posters. Log on to **www.scholastic.com**, or call 1-800-SCHOLASTIC.

Sports Illustrated for Kids

Many second- and third-graders love to write about sports, and this publication provides current information about athletes, safety, trends, and more. Log on to **www.sikids.com**, or call 1-800-833-1661.

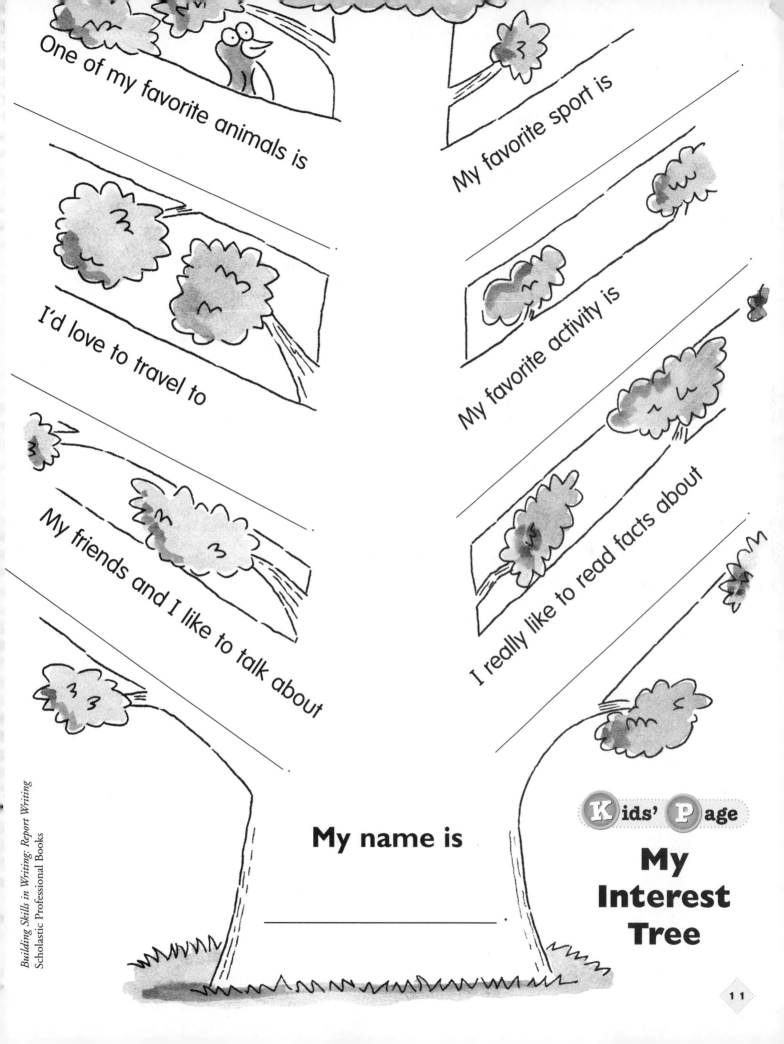

One of my favorite animals is

My favorite sport is

I'd love to travel to

My favorite activity is

My friends and I like to talk about

I really like to read facts about

My name is

Kids' **P**age

My Interest Tree

Building Skills in Writing: Report Writing
Scholastic Professional Books

STEP 2

Materials

- copy of Kids' Page 14 for each student
- scissors
- tape or glue sticks

Checking Scope

Topic-Shrinking Machine

(Use with Kids' Page 14.)

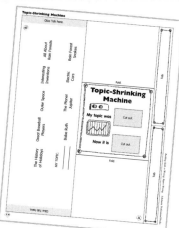

Once students have brainstormed potential topics, check to see if the topics are focused enough for a second- or third-grade report. If a topic is too broad, the student will likely find too much information and will have a tough time organizing it into a cohesive report. On the other hand, if a topic is too narrow, students may not be able to dig up enough details to support the main idea. For example:

Topics That Are Probably Too Broad:

- ◎ The Age of Dinosaurs
- ◎ All About Soccer
- ◎ Dogs

Topics That Are Probably Too Narrow:

- ◎ How a Maiasaurus Protected Its Eggs
- ◎ Who Won World Cup 2001
- ◎ What to Feed a Dog

Topics That Are Just Right in Scope:

- ◎ How Dinos Raised Their Babies
- ◎ Soccer's World Cup
- ◎ How to Care for a Pet Dog

I have noticed that most children need help reigning in a too-big topic rather than expanding a too-focused one. You can use the reproducible on page 14 to provide practice in making topics more focused. Here's how:

1 Provide each student with a copy of the Topic-Shrinking Machine reproducible on page 14.

2 Tell students to cut out the two panels—panel A, the shrinking machine, and panel B, the topic strip. Then have students color panel A.

3 Direct students to cut out the two windows from panel A (the machine). To do this, show them how to fold the panel at a right angle to the dotted lines. Then have them snip along the lines from the crease of the fold inward.

4 Have students fold the machine inward along the solid lines and tape it closed.

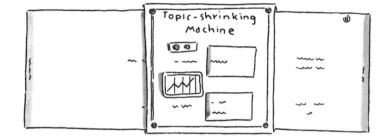

5 Next, show students how to slide the topic strip (panel B) through the machine.

6 To keep the topic strip from accidentally sliding out of the machine and getting lost, have students cut out the two small rectangular tabs on the reproducible. Have them tape or glue one tab to each end of the strip.

7 To use the slider, direct students to pull the left side of the topic strip all the way to the left. Then, as they pull the strip to the right, they can watch as each topic magically appears in the windows of the machine.

8 In the final step of this activity, students try their own hand at "shrinking" a topic. Invite them to write a new report topic in the space provided when it appears in the machine window. Students' answers will vary. Have students share the specific holiday topics they choose.

Keep in mind that even with teacher assistance, it's not uncommon for students to reach the drafting stage of a report before realizing that a topic is too broad or too narrow. Point out that it's never too late to fine-tune one's topic; it will only make for a better report!

Topic-Shrinking Machine

Glue Tab here.

B

All About Rain Forests

Rain Forest Snakes

Interesting Inventions

Electric Cars

Outer Space

The Planet Jupiter

Great Baseball Players

Babe Ruth

The History of Holidays

MY TOPIC:

_____

_____

Fold.

Topic-Shrinking Machine

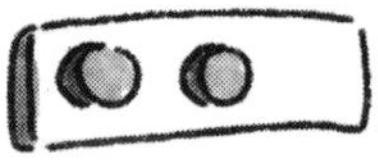

My topic was

Cut out.

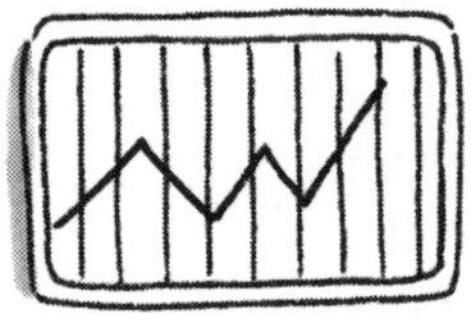

Now it is

Cut out.

Fold.

Tab

Tab

A

Glue Tab here.

Building Skills in Writing: Report Writing   Scholastic Professional Books

Forming Research Questions

Bright-Beginnings Report Planner

(Use with Kids' Pages 17 and 18.)

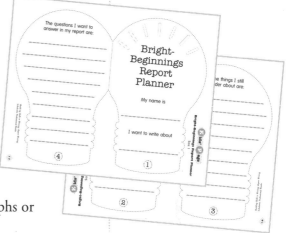

Once students have settled on topics that are appropriate in scope, they should assess what they already know about their subjects and list specific questions to answer in their reports. I recommend having students choose two to three questions for their reports, depending on the scope of the questions and the length of the report you have in mind. Using questions as a starting point for research provides a clear focus for beginning researchers and makes it easier for them to organize the information they uncover. Once students' research is complete, the questions can be adapted to serve as the main ideas of paragraphs or sections in the students' reports.

This activity is an easy way to help students fine-tune their topics and focus on what they really want to learn. In it, students will make a mini-book to guide them through the process of developing research questions. The mini-book asks students to think about and write down:

- ◎ the topic they would like to write about.

- ◎ what they already know about the topic.

- ◎ any questions they still wonder about.

- ◎ which questions they would like to answer in their report.

Here's how to make it:

1 Give each student a copy of the Bright-Beginnings Report Planner reproducible. (NOTE: Make double-sided copies of pages 17 and 18 so the lightbulb patterns line up back to back.) Tell students to cut out the pattern along the outer dotted lines.

2 Next, have students fold their planner along the vertical solid line to make a four-page mini-book.

Here's an example of how the planner can help a student come up with specific research questions. A student might write:

- ◎ I want to write a report about chocolate because I love it!

- ◎ I know that chocolate tastes good and can be in candy and cakes and ice cream. I know that chocolate comes from some kind of bean. I know you should not eat too much chocolate because it's bad for your teeth.

Materials

- • double-sided copy of Kids' Pages 17 and 18 for each student
- • scissors

◎ I still wonder: Where does chocolate come from? Can I grow it in my backyard? How does it get turned into candy? Why is there milk chocolate and dark chocolate? Do people everywhere eat chocolate? When and how did people first eat chocolate?

◎ In my report, I have decided to answer the questions: Where does chocolate come from? How does chocolate get turned into candy?

Once students have completed their Bright-Beginnings Report Planner, meet briefly with each student for a writing-progress check. Discuss students' chosen focus, and get the research process rolling by asking students where they think they might find the answers to their questions. You should also begin tracking each student's progress in the writing process. Plan to meet regularly with each student to look at his or her work to-date and to discuss any problems. You can use the checklist on page 19 to record when students pass each report-writing milestone.

Some things I already know about my topic are:

I know that bridges let cars and trains go across rivers and oceans. I know that there are different kinds of bridges. I know that bridges are sometimes made of steel.

②

Some things I still wonder about are:

How do bridges work? What makes them stay up? Why are there different kinds of bridges? What's the longest bridge in the world? Why do bridges sway when it's windy?

③

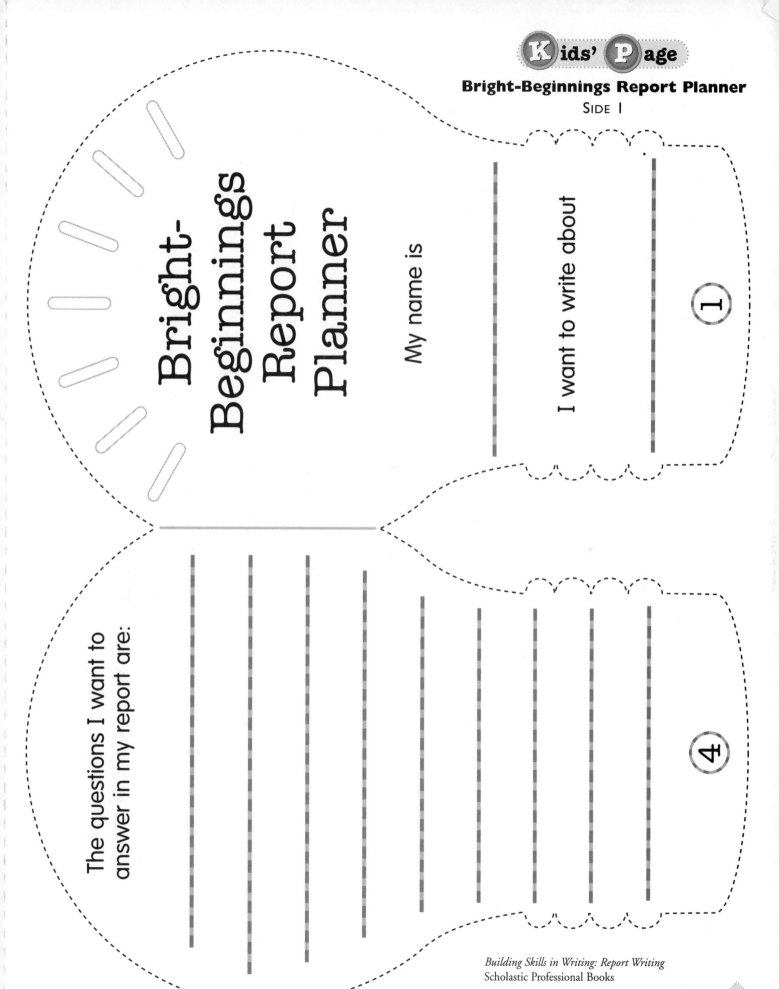

Bright-Beginnings Report Planner

My name is

I want to write about

1

The questions I want to answer in my report are:

4

Building Skills in Writing: Report Writing
Scholastic Professional Books

17

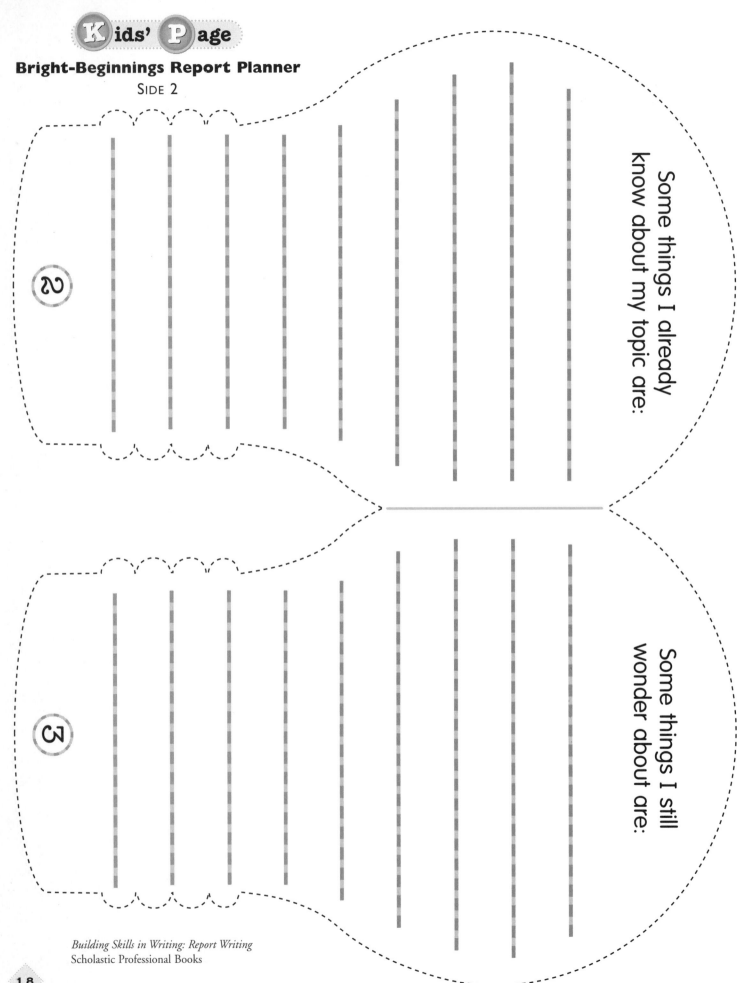

2

Some things I already
know about my topic are:

3

Some things I still
wonder about are:

Tracking Student Progress

Meet periodically with each student to gauge his or her progress. Put a date in the grid to show when the student completes each task.

Name	Selected a topic	Identified research questions	Found sources of information	Took notes	Wrote draft of report	Revised report	Edited report	Published final version

Research and Note-Taking

I magine dumping a few thousand books in the middle of your classroom floor, then poring through the mess for a specific bit of data. To young students with little or no experience in navigating libraries, that's how the start of the research process can feel.

In their first year or two of elementary school, your students probably did not need to find many resources on their own. Now, in order to write their first real research reports, they will need to decipher the Dewey decimal system; use encyclopedias, indexes, and tables of contents; fine-tune Internet search strategies; learn to take notes as they read; and more. Your challenge is to introduce these research and note-taking skills in a way that is stimulating, not scary. The suggestions and activities in this section will help you get started.

Top Six Student Misconceptions About Research

As you introduce the research process, keep in mind these common misconceptions—and help your students move past them!

Myth 1: You always have to read the whole book—even if the topic you're researching is contained only in one chapter.

The truth is, it depends on the book. In some cases, reading the whole book may merely confuse a child by introducing irrelevant information. For example, if a student is researching giant pandas and finds a chapter book on endangered animals, he or she can probably read just the chapter on pandas. On the other hand, if a student is researching lunar eclipses and finds a short book about the moon, I would recommend that he or she skim the whole book, paying special attention to sections that discuss eclipses. Don't feel as if you're encouraging students to cheat or cut corners by focusing only on the materials that pertain to their topics. As any editor will tell you, one trait of a talented researcher is the ability to locate information quickly and efficiently. In fact, that's why book publishers provide tables of contents, indexes, and other guides.

Myth 2: If you put it in your own words, you don't need to give credit to the source.

Yes, you do! There are two things every student should know about "borrowing" information from books and other sources. First, it's important to put the information into one's own words (unless using a direct quote). And second, unless the topic is something students have studied or witnessed firsthand, they should include a list of works they consulted for the report. While you don't need to require high-school level bibliographies, it's a good idea to have students keep track of the sources they used and include a list of these sources with their reports. Why? This ensures that students can go back and check facts later if a mistake is suspected. It also teaches students to respect other writers' hard work. And it gets students in the habit of documenting their research so that this practice won't come as a big surprise later.

Myth 3: Once you've found a book or Web site on your topic, you can stop researching.

Not a good idea. To research a topic thoroughly, each student should consult at least two or three sources. You may require even more than that, depending on the sort of research students are doing. Each author approaches the topic from a unique perspective; your students can gain a lot by reading and comparing several of those perspectives.

Myth 4: Any old book will do.

Unfortunately, not all children's books are top-caliber. Many libraries have directed the lion's share of their funding over the past several years to computer-age projects such as electronic card catalogs and increased Internet access. Without question, these improvements help make research a breeze for today's second- and third-graders. But there is an insidious flip side: Less money may be spent on current nonfiction books. Take a peak at your library's titles and you may discover very outdated books. Check copyright dates and skim the books to see if the information is still accurate. In many cases, an old book is still a good book. But in a few instances, an outdated book can lead to a report filled with inaccuracies or stereotypes.

Myth 5: It's cheating if you ask for help. AND its axillary,
Myth 6: Librarians are there to do the work for you.

My librarian friends tell me it's time to debunk both of these. Some students are shy about asking for assistance using the card catalog or search engines or hunting for a title in the stacks. As a result, they do inefficient searches, grow frustrated quickly, and leave the library thinking there are no resources on their subject. Other kids are budding couch potatoes; they enter a library, tell the staff their topic, and expect the librarians to do most of the work. Tell your class that librarians are available to help children find the information they need but not to do the work for them. For example, students can ask a librarian to demonstrate how to do a subject search on the computer but not to do repeated searches for them.

Teaching Research and Note-Taking

The following strategies and suggestions are organized into four categories: Library Research, Internet Research, Interviews and Surveys, and Note-Taking. Check the end of each section for reproducibles that will help make implementing the strategies a snap.

Introducing Library Research

STRATEGY 1: Map the Library

Take students on a tour of the school or local library. But try not to overwhelm them; focus on just a few of the basic resources they will need, including the card catalog, encyclopedias, and nonfiction stacks. (If at all possible, visit the library several times and introduce one resource or section per visit.) Invite students to draw simple maps of the library, showing where these resources are located.

STRATEGY 2: Explore Call Numbers

(Use with Kids' Page 24.)

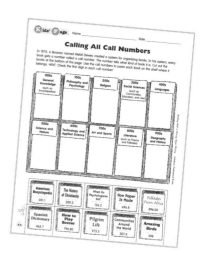

Demonstrate how the Dewey decimal system works. Have students use the Calling All Call Numbers reproducible to keep track of how the subject areas are grouped. Keep in mind, however, that it may be some time before most students can consistently locate a book by its call number. For a while, you and your librarian will need to help. As you assist students, model how to approach the task. For example, say: "The book you're looking for is 101.52, so I know it will come after this one, with the call number 101.34."

Materials

- copy of Kids' Page 24 for each student

STRATEGY 3: Teach Search Secrets

Practice doing searches for nonfiction books by title, author, and subject. Remind students that correct spelling is essential when doing computer searches (most libraries now have electronic card catalogs). Also keep in mind that a subject or key word search can be especially challenging for young students, since it is sometimes tricky to figure out the exact string of words that will produce the desired results. At the same time, this is the type of search students will need to conduct most often when writing research reports. Help students brainstorm synonyms and related subject words for various topics.

STRATEGY 4: **Take Advantage of a Book's Tools**

(Use with Kids' Page 25.)

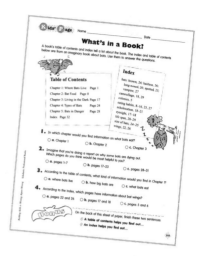

Using an on-level nonfiction book (or one of your students' content-area textbooks), demonstrate how to use a table of contents and an index. Explain that these features make it possible to get to information very quickly. Be sure to point out that in an index, a dash between page numbers means that everything between those pages is included. A comma between page numbers means that only the two pages listed—not the pages in between—include information on that topic. The What's in a Book? reproducible on page 25 lets your students practice using a table of contents and an index.

Materials

● copy of Kids' Page 25 for each student

STRATEGY 5: **Passport-to-Research Mini-Book**

(Use with Kids' Page 26.)

To encourage your students to become familiar with all types of resources (nonfiction books, periodicals, encyclopedias, Internet sites, and so on), require that they use each type at least once. The Passport-to-Research reproducible is a fun way for students to keep track of which sources they have consulted and which ones they still need to explore. With this activity, students make a "passport" and give themselves a "stamp" for each resource type they use. Keep in mind that your students may not need to consult all types of resources in the course of researching a single report. However, once they've written two or three reports, students should have utilized all of them.

   To make the passport mini-books, simply have students cut out the pages along the dotted lines, put the pages in numerical order with the cover on top, and staple the left side of the passports. To give the passports an official air, you might ask students to get each entry or page stamped by you or by the library staff. Once everyone has at least one entry per page, consider throwing a travel theme party to celebrate how much students have learned about the research process.

Materials

● copy of Kids' Page 26 for each student
● scissors
● stapler

Calling All Call Numbers

In 1873, a librarian named Melvil Dewey created a system for organizing books. In his system, every book gets a number called a call number. The number tells what kind of book it is. Cut out the books at the bottom of the page. Use the call numbers to paste each book on the shelf where it belongs. HINT: Check the first digit in each call number!

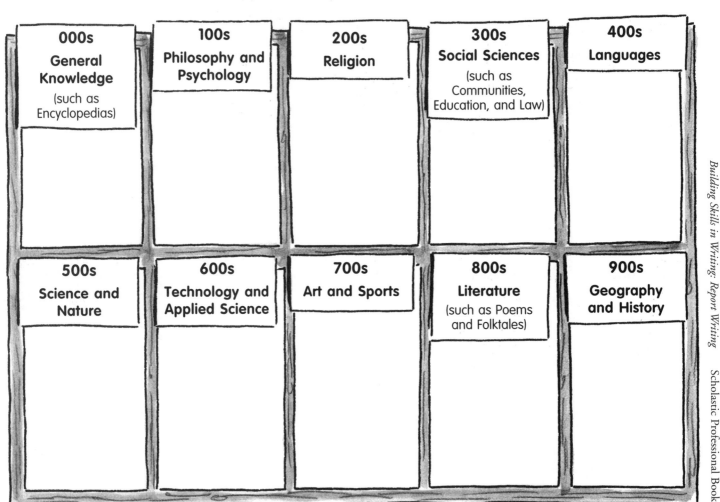

000s General Knowledge (such as Encyclopedias)

100s Philosophy and Psychology

200s Religion

300s Social Sciences (such as Communities, Education, and Law)

400s Languages

500s Science and Nature

600s Technology and Applied Science

700s Art and Sports

800s Literature (such as Poems and Folktales)

900s Geography and History

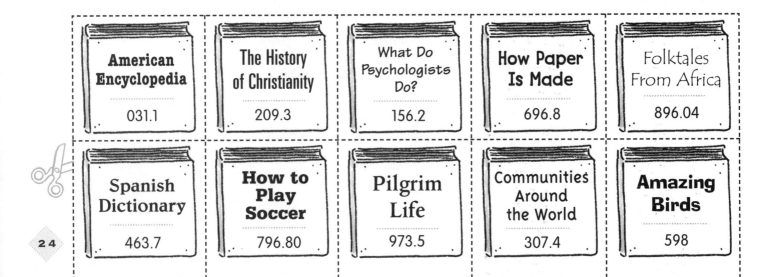

American Encyclopedia	The History of Christianity	What Do Psychologists Do?	How Paper Is Made	Folktales From Africa
031.1	209.3	156.2	696.8	896.04
Spanish Dictionary	How to Play Soccer	Pilgrim Life	Communities Around the World	Amazing Birds
463.7	796.80	973.5	307.4	598

Building Skills in Writing: Report Writing

Scholastic Professional Books

What's in a Book?

A book's table of contents and index tell a lot about the book. The index and table of contents below are from an imaginary book about bats. Use them to answer the questions.

Table of Contents

Index

1. In which chapter would you find information on what bats eat?

○ **a.** Chapter 1   ○ **b.** Chapter 2   ○ **c.** Chapter 3

2. Imagine that you're doing a report on why some bats are dying out. Which pages do you think would be most helpful to you?

○ **a.** pages 1–7   ○ **b.** pages 17–23   ○ **c.** pages 28–31

3. According to the table of contents, what kind of information would you find in Chapter 1?

○ **a.** where bats live   ○ **b.** how big bats are   ○ **c.** what bats eat

4. According to the index, which pages have information about bat wings?

○ **a.** pages 22 and 26   ○ **b.** pages 17 and 18   ○ **c.** pages 5 and 6

On the back of this sheet of paper, finish these two sentences:

◎ **A table of contents helps you find out...**

◎ **An index helps you find out...**

Passport-to-Research Mini-Book

PASSPORT TO RESEARCH

Use this book to keep track of the places you find information. Write the title of each resource on the page where it belongs.

Name _____

① 1

I used these nonfiction books:
(Write the title and author.)

② 2

I used these encyclopedia articles:
(Write the encyclopedia name and title of article.)

③ 3

I talked to these people:
(Write the names of people you interviewed or surveyed and the dates when you talked to them.)

I used these Internet sites:
(Write the Web address and the name of the group that sponsors the site.)

④ 4

I used these magazine and newspaper articles:
(Write the name of the magazine or newspaper, the issue date, page number, and the title of the article.)

⑤ 5

⑥ 6

Building Skills in Writing: Report Writing   Scholastic Professional Books

Introducing Internet Research

You'll probably find that many of your students are more adept at finding sites on the Internet than they are at hunting down a book in the library stacks! Many of today's kids have been wielding a mouse and keyboard since they were preschoolers. However, until now, your students have probably been using the Internet primarily as a source of games and activities. They have not needed to surf sites looking for specific information. Because they are new at this—and because inappropriate material can literally be just a click away, I suggest that you preview research sites in advance and bookmark appropriate ones on your classroom computer. ("Bookmarking" means naming a site as one of your favorite places. When students click on your list of bookmarked sites, they simply need to scroll down to the one that matches their subject area.) If that's not possible, make yourself available at the time students are conducting their Internet research. Visit with each researcher to help him or her search for sites and to make sure the sites he or she is using are suitable.

Below are some kid-friendly sites to get students started. For criteria to use when evaluating other sites for potential student use, see the checklist on page 28.

Sites to See: Recommended Web Sites for Students

HOLIDAYS AROUND THE WORLD
www.kidlink.org/KIDPROJ/MCC/
Find background, customs, recipes, and more. This site is created by kids for kids.

INVENTORS HALL OF FAME
www.invent.org
Biographies of some of the greatest inventors of all time.

NATIONAL WILDLIFE FEDERATION
www.nwf.org/kids/
Information on environmental issues such as wetlands, animals, and more.

SCIENCE AND NATURE FOR KIDS
www.kidscience.about.com/kids/kidscience
Research everything from health and nutrition to animal habitats.

THE WHITE HOUSE
www.whitehouse.gov/WH/kids/
Information about Presidents, first ladies, White House history, and more.

NATIONAL AERONAUTICS AND SPACE ADMINISTRATION (NASA)
www.kids.msfc.nasa.gov/
Facts about astronauts, space missions, the International Space Station, and more.

SAN DIEGO ZOO
www.sandiegozoo.org
Find out how much a hippo weighs, what okapis eat for lunch, and other fascinating facts!

NATURAL DISASTERS
www.fema.gov/kids/lib
Search this site for information on hurricanes, earthquakes, and tornadoes.

DISCOVERY KIDS
www.kids.discovery.com/KIDS/home
Offers sections on dinosaurs, technology, and "yucky" stuff like sweating and burping.

RAIN FOREST ACTION NETWORK
www.ran.org/kids_action/index1.html
Information about people and animals that inhabit the rain forest, as well as information about conservation for both children and teachers.

Finding Appropriate Web Sites for Students

◯ Does the site provide information on its authorship/sponsorship? If not, check the address. Sites hosted by the federal government—including sites such as the postal service and White House—have ".gov" in their addresses. Commercial sites, such as those hosted by Scholastic and other businesses, have ".com," whereas sites from non-profit organizations often include ".org." College and university sites usually contain ".edu." Sites hosted by individuals usually have a tilde (~) in the address. Be aware that content may be less reliable on personal Web sites, since you know little if anything about the creator.

◯ Is there plenty of information within the site itself? Although links can prove useful, you should probably avoid sites that act primarily as links to other sites. It is easy for students to get lost when clicking on link after link, as well as get sent to inappropriate sites.

◯ Is the text on-level and easy to read? A good children's site avoids distracting type styles, backgrounds, and graphics.

◯ Is the content well-organized and easy to navigate? Look for things like simple headlines with related icons for students to click on; such features make it easier for children to navigate.

◯ Is the content current? Especially when hunting for sites on time-sensitive issues, check to see when the site was last updated (many sites include this information).

◯ Does the site load relatively quickly? Sites with elaborate graphics can sometimes take an interminable time to appear onscreen. Your students may grow frustrated—or even run out of research time before they've found anything useful. Some sites offer two versions at the start, one which lets you avoid slow-loading animation.

◯ Do you have all of the required "plug-ins"? There is nothing worse than finding a promising site, then discovering that you can't use it because you don't have the software needed for its sound or animation files! Most sites will prompt you to download any missing plug-ins; make sure you do so before directing students to them.

◯ Is the site free of obvious spelling and grammatical mistakes? When careless errors appear on a site, one can't help but wonder what other mistakes or inaccuracies the site contains. Reputable organizations generally screen their content very carefully before posting it.

◯ Can students use the site anonymously and without paying a fee? Be wary of sites that require a membership fee or ask users to type in their names and e-mail addresses. If a free site requires you to "register" by giving a name or e-mail address, create a class username and/or password ahead of time, and give to students—never allow children to enter their own names or home e-mail addresses.

Building Skills in Writing: Report Writing

Scholastic Professional Books

Introducing Interviews and Surveys

While secondary sources such as books and Internet sites will serve your students well for most research reports, students may occasionally need to collect primary data in the form of interviews or surveys. For example, if a student is writing about the Mexican celebration of Las Posadas, she might want to interview a fellow student or community member who was born in Mexico and can share memories of this holiday. Depending on the topic, quotes and anecdotes from interviews can often help a research report come alive.

Interviewing Checklist to Share With Students

◎ Explain why you are doing the interview.

◎ Ask questions that the person can't answer with a yes or no.

◎ Good question-starters include "Why did you…," "How did you…," and "Can you tell me a little about…."

◎ Look at the person often during the interview. Smile!

◎ Take careful notes.

◎ Ask the person to repeat what he or she said if you need to.

Students may also conduct simple surveys to collect quantitative information on a given topic. For example, if a student is researching scooter popularity, he may poll his classmates to find out how many children actually own scooters. Since tallying responses can be difficult and time-consuming, I'd suggest limiting second- and third-graders to surveys with one or two basic questions. And unless students are working in small groups to conduct their surveys, I'd advise sticking with sample sizes of no more than 25 or 30 people. While college-level researchers need to worry about a large enough sample for statistical purposes, your students are just getting their feet wet when it comes to research. The idea is to stir up some excitement and get them interested in various ways of gathering data.

Surveying Checklist to Share With Students

◎ Ask only one or two questions.

◎ Make your question(s) multiple choice.

◎ Use questions that can be answered with one word, such as yes or no.

◎ Good question-starters include "Do you…," "How often do you…," and "Which one of these do you…."

◎ Decide whom you want to survey (for example, second-graders, school bus riders, kids who eat school lunches), and stick to that group.

◎ Keep answers organized by making a chart before you set out to give the survey. When a person answers your question, record the answer with a check mark or an "X" in the appropriate section of your chart.

Do You Own a Scooter?		
Name	Yes	No

Introducing Note-Taking

Once students have a good idea of where to locate the information they need, help them learn to take notes as they go. Good note-taking is a prerequisite for effective report-writing because it helps the writer remember details accurately and organize information. Encourage students to keep notes short and to the point, to focus on the important ideas, and to put notes in their own words. Some additional note-taking strategies follow.

STRATEGY 1: **Use a Grid**

(Use with Kids' Pages 31 and 32.)

Help students realize that note-taking is a way to stay focused on one's research questions and not get overly sidetracked by irrelevant information. To that end, many researchers create a page for each subtopic or research question, then write on that page only notes pertaining to that question. Another approach is to have students create a grid listing their research questions and then record answers to those research questions on the grid. On page 31, you'll find a reproducible designed to get students started in the grid-making process. Distribute the All the Answers reproducible and show students how to write their research questions across the top of the grid. Then have them list their information sources along the left-hand side. As students exhaust each source, have them use the grid to record what the source says about each research question. A completed grid helps students see several things at a glance: (1) whether they have sufficiently answered each research question; (2) which source provided which bit of information; and (3) whether sources are in agreement on the answers to the research questions.

Remind students that it is important to include with their reports the names of books and other resources that they used in their research. The Name Your Sources reproducible on page 32 shows one way of listing each type of material.

STRATEGY 2: **Make a Web**

(Use with Kids' Page 33.)

For many young students, organizing notes on a web is easier than making an outline. Show students how to record the main idea and supporting details of a book, Internet site, or article on the Big Deal Note-Taking Wheel reproducible on page 33.

Materials

- copies of Kids' Pages 31 and 32 for each student

Materials

- copy of Kids' Page 33 for each student

Kids' Page

All the Answers

Write your questions across the top of the chart. Write your sources (books, Web sites, and other places you find information) down the left side of the chart. In the middle of the chart, write what each source says about each question.

	Question 1:	Question 2:
Source		
Source		
Source		

Building Skills in Writing: Report Writing   Scholastic Professional Books

Name Your Sources

It's important to name the books and other materials you used to write your report. These examples show one way to list each type of material.

Books

Name the title, author, publishing company, and the year the book was published.

Amazing Spiders, by Claudia Schnieper (Carolrhoda Books, 1989).

Internet Sites

Name the site's title (or creator) and address.

The White House Web site, www.whitehouse.gov.

Encyclopedias

Name the encyclopedia series, article title, page number, and the year it was published.

Learning Encyclopedia, "Amphibians," page 43. 1999.

Interviews

Name the person you spoke with and the date you spoke with him or her.

Interview with Larry Stevens, owner of Stevens Bakery, April 19, 2002.

Surveys

Tell whom you surveyed and when you did it.

Survey of 25 third-graders at Wilson School, October 2002.

Building Skills in Writing: Report Writing

Scholastic Professional Books

Big Deal Note-Taking Wheel

Use this wheel to take notes about your report topic. In the middle of the wheel, write your research question. On each spoke, write information from your research that helps answer your question.

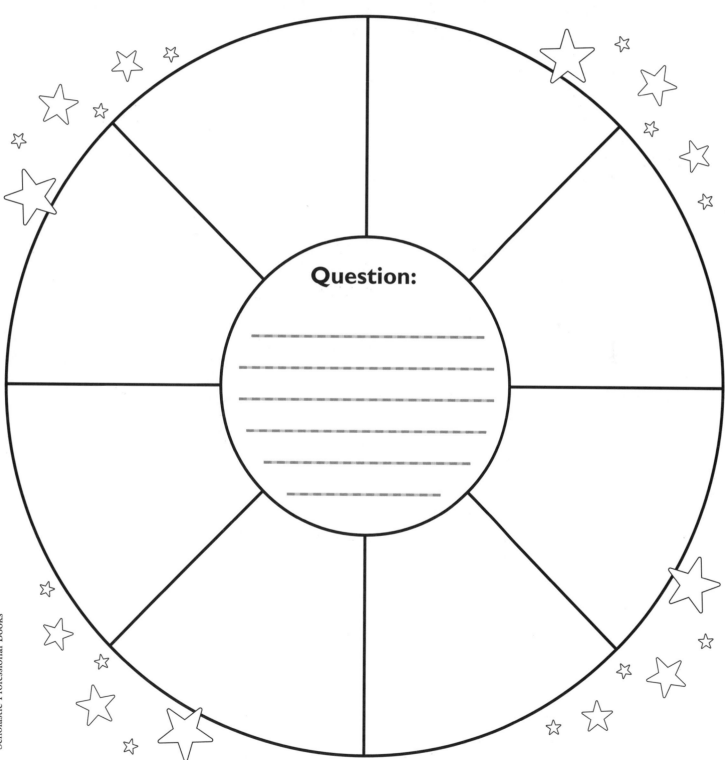

Question:

Building Skills in Writing: Report Writing
Scholastic Professional Books

3

Turning Notes Into A-Plus Reports

By this point your students are so immersed in their report topics that they're probably spouting facts and figures to anyone who will listen. The next step is to capture those thoughts on paper and create a draft of the report. This section has lessons designed to give students guidance and practice in the report-drafting stage, from creating catchy beginnings to keeping all that information organized.

You'll also find lessons and suggestions aimed at helping students liven up their report formats. Although there's nothing wrong with a traditional two-page report, you can easily jazz things up with creative formats like cereal-box reports, question-and-answer mini-books, and classroom-produced magazines.

The Editing My Report checklist on page 54 details the report-writing strategies students will learn about in this chapter. Use it to organize your lessons, and make copies for students to use as a writing/revision checklist.

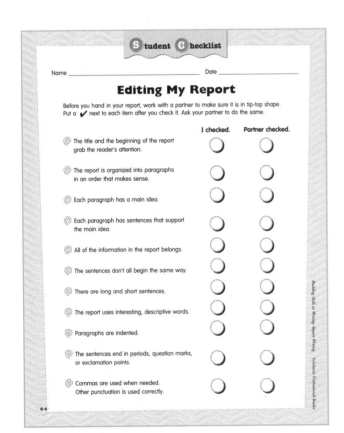

Great-Opening-Acts Flap Book

WRITING SKILLS Students will explore several ways to begin a report.

A great lead, or beginning, draws readers in like an ice cream truck draws kids on a hot summer day. It catches the readers' attention and introduces the topic of the report in a succinct fashion. But writing great beginnings is not a skill that comes easily to most young writers. Many of them simply begin their reports with the first piece of information that catches their eye. In this activity, students will read and try their hand at several styles of report beginnings, then decide which works best for their particular topic.

Prewriting

◎ Make sure each student has identified a clear report topic and researched the topic thoroughly.

◎ To expose students to different kinds of nonfiction openers, include well-written nonfiction titles when you read aloud.

Writing and Revising

1 Have students cut out each page of the Great-Opening Acts flap book (each is a different size) and compile the pages in numerical order. Direct students to align the pages along the top edge and staple to bind the book.

2 Tell students to turn to each labeled section to read examples of each type of report beginning: summary sentences, questions, and scene setters.

3 In the space provided, have students write at least one draft of each type of report beginning. They should use their own report topics.

4 Have students pair up to discuss which "opening act" each student favors most for his or her actual report. Students can trade opinions and advice for making the openers more lively and effective. Afterward, meet briefly with each student to find out which style he or she has chosen and why. (NOTE: It's fine for students to use other kinds of openings not covered in the flap book.)

5 Some students will want to use the flap-book framework each time they need to write a report beginning. Consider making clean copies of the flap book available each time you assign a report.

Editing and Publishing

Have students incorporate their favorite beginnings into their reports. As students revise and edit their work as a whole, they may need to edit their beginnings.

Materials

● copies of Kids' Pages 36 and 37 for each student
● scissors
● crayons or markers
● stapler

A **summary sentence** defines your topic or gives your main idea right at the top of your report.

Examples

Americans have been enjoying basketball for more than 100 years. This sport was invented in Massachusetts back in 1891.

Comets are chunks of ice, dust, or rock. They travel very quickly around the Sun.

Write your own summary sentence:

_____

_____

_____

_____

_____

_____

 Summarize Your Main Idea   ②

Building Skills in Writing: Report Writing   Scholastic Professional Books

Starting with a **question** can get readers thinking about your topic.

(**Examples**)

Are you afraid of spiders? Many people are. They don't know that most spiders are harmless.

Did you ever wonder how we got our national anthem? It all started with a poet named Francis Scott Key.

Write your own opening question:

_____

_____

_____

_____

_____

_____

☆ **Ask a Question** ☆ ③

You can also start your report by **setting the scene**, or asking readers to imagine your topic.

(**Examples**)

Picture yourself digging for hours under a hot desert sun. That's what paleontologists, or dinosaur experts, do.

The year was 1787. The place was Philadelphia, Pennsylvania. Representatives from the 13 colonies met to plan our nation's Constitution.

Write your own scene-setter:

_____

_____

_____

_____

_____

_____

 Set the Scene   ④

What's the Scoop?

WRITING SKILLS Students will build paragraphs by matching supporting details to main ideas.

In this activity students will practice matching supporting details to a main idea. Then they will use what they've learned to write their own paragraph.

Prewriting

◎ Distribute the What's the Scoop? reproducible and have students cut the page in half along the dotted line. As a prewriting exercise, they'll be working with the preprinted ice cream cone and scoops on the top half of the page.

◎ Read aloud the main idea on the ice cream cone. Instruct students to cut out the cone and the four ice cream scoops. Students should then paste the cone onto a sheet of construction paper. On top of the cone, have them arrange only those scoops that go with the main idea. Then they can glue them on the cone in an order that makes sense. To make the activity easier, reveal that there are three scoops that support the main idea. To make the activity more challenging, keep that clue to yourself!

Writing and Revising

1 Have students cut out the blank ice cream cone and scoops on the bottom of the page. On the cone, students can write a main idea for one of their report paragraphs.

2 Ask students to write supporting details for their main ideas on the blank ice cream scoops. They can then stack the scoops atop the cone in an order that makes sense, and paste the cone and scoops into place on a sheet of construction paper and color the whole creation.

3 Have students rewrite the main idea and supporting details in paragraph form.

Editing and Publishing

Have students check their spelling and punctuation before creating final drafts. Show off students' work by posting their original cones on an ice-cream-themed bulletin board titled, "Here's the Scoop on Paragraphs."

Materials

- copy of Kids' Page 39 for each student
- scissors
- glue sticks
- construction paper

What's the Scoop?

Cut out all the pieces. Find the details that go with the main idea. (HINT: Not all of them do!) Put them together to make an ice cream cone.

Main Idea: Ice cream cones were invented in 1903 by a man named Italo Marchiony.

Detail: He sold lemon ices in New York City.

Detail: Chocolate is a popular ice cream flavor.

Detail: He wanted an easy way to serve the icy treats.

Detail: He tried serving ices in paper cones. Then he began making cones that people could eat.

It's your turn! Write a main idea on the cone. On the scoops write details that support the main idea. Paste them together.

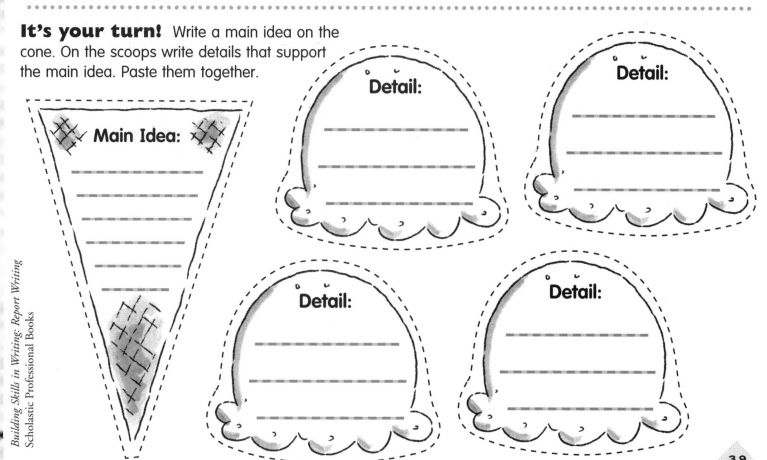

Main Idea: _____

Detail: _____

Detail: _____

Detail: _____

Detail: _____

What Doesn't Belong?

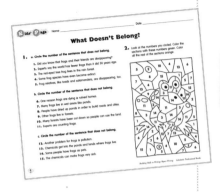

WRITING SKILLS **WRITING SKILLS** Students will learn to exclude irrelevant details from their reports.

Picture this: You're reading a student report on dolphin communication, pleased at the student's thorough research and vivid descriptions. Suddenly, from out of the blue you happen upon a sentence or two about seals. *Where did this come from?* The truth is, it can be hard for students to edit out information they find interesting, even if the information is not directly related to the report topic.

In this activity students will explore the role that supporting details play in a report. Explain that supporting details have this name because they support, or give more information about, the main idea. As this activity demonstrates, details that do not support the main idea of a paragraph can confuse the reader and should be left out. These details may fit better in a different section of the report, or they may not belong in the report at all.

Prewriting

◎ Read aloud two or three nonfiction paragraphs in which there are strong main ideas. As you read, toss in a sentence on a slightly different topic. After each paragraph, ask students what was wrong with the way the paragraph was written. When students respond that, "The part about _____ didn't belong," discuss why that might be a problem for a reader.

Writing and Revising

1 Before students write their own paragraphs, have them read the examples on the What Doesn't Belong? reproducible on page 41. Students should identify the number of the sentence that does not belong in each group.

2 Allow time for students to complete the color-by-numbers portion of the page—a fun way for them to check their work. Students should use the directions to decide how to color each space. If they've deleted the correct sentences from Part 1, they'll end up with a picture of a frog!

3 Have students choose a topic and write an original paragraph on the back of the reproducible. Each paragraph should have a clearly stated main idea and three or more supporting details. For each detail they add, remind students to ask themselves the question, "Does this sentence tell more about the main idea?"

Editing

Have students trade papers and evaluate each other's paragraphs. Do all of the sentences belong? Why or why not?

Materials

● copy of Kids' Page 41 for each student

● crayons or markers

What Doesn't Belong?

1.

a. Circle the number of the sentence that does not belong.

1. Did you know that frogs and their friends are disappearing?

2. Experts say the world has fewer frogs than it did 50 years ago.

3. The red-eyed tree frog lives in the rain forest.

4. Some frog species have even become extinct.

5. Frog relatives, like toads and salamanders, are disappearing, too.

b. Circle the number of the sentence that does not belong.

6. One reason frogs are dying is ruined homes.

7. Many frogs live in wet areas like ponds.

8. People have dried up ponds in order to build roads and cities.

9. Other frogs live in forests.

10. Many forests have been cut down so people can use the land.

11. Experts are counting frogs.

c. Circle the number of the sentence that does not belong.

12. Another problem for frogs is pollution.

13. Chemicals get into the ponds and lands where frogs live.

14. Some people have frogs as pets.

15. The chemicals can make frogs very sick.

2. Look at the numbers you circled. Color the sections with these numbers green. Color all the rest of the sections orange.

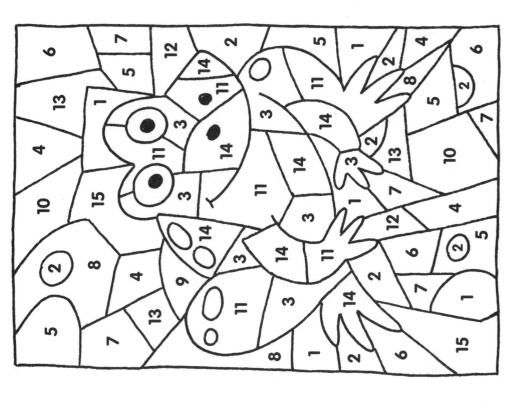

Building Skills in Writing: Report Writing   Scholastic Professional Books

Order in the Report! Paragraph Game

WRITING SKILLS Students will learn to organize reports by putting paragraphs in their appropriate sequence.

Materials

- copy of Kids' Page 43 for each student
- 3- by 5-inch index cards
- sheets of 8 1/2- by 14-inch legal paper
- glue sticks
- stapler (optional)

By now, your students have written rough drafts of the paragraphs that will make up their reports. At this point it is important to make sure the paragraphs are arranged in an order that makes sense. In this activity students will practice sequencing paragraphs. Then they'll apply what they've learned about sequencing to their own reports.

Prewriting

◎ Read aloud several nonfiction passages. Talk about why each writer may have chosen to put his or her ideas in that particular order. Are ideas arranged chronologically? In order of importance? Make a list of possible ways to organize information.

Writing and Revising

1 Invite each student to cut out the cards on the Order in the Report! reproducible and arrange them in order. If you'd like, have students number the cards, staple them together, and create a cover to make a mini-book about the Turtle Hospital.

2 Direct students to write paragraphs that answer their research questions on index cards. Then have students play with the order of the cards until the sequence feels right to them. Once each student has ordered his or her cards, provide large sheets of paper on which students can glue their cards.

3 Now students will need to revise their paragraphs to reflect the chosen order of information. For example, they may need to change the beginnings of some paragraphs to make transitions smoother or rewrite the last part of the last paragraph so that it helps to sum up the whole report. Seeing the paragraphs laid out on the desk should help students pinpoint areas that need revision.

Editing and Publishing

Have students edit and proofread their paragraphs and then create final, polished versions of their reports. Instead of having students type their reports on the computer or copy the reports onto fresh looseleaf paper, consider having them make polished versions of their paragraph cards. They can add artwork to the reverse side and present the cards to the whole class as a projector-free slide show.

Building Skills in Writing: Report Writing   Scholastic Professional Books

Doctors at the Turtle Hospital treat hundreds of sick turtles every year. Many patients are sea turtles that have been hit by boats. Other patients are turtles that have gotten tangled in fishing lines.

This is card number

You may have been to a hospital before, but you've never seen one like the Turtle Hospital. It's a hospital just for sea turtles. It's in Marathon, Florida.

This is card number

Most sea turtles stay at the Turtle Hospital for a year. While they're getting better, they swim inside a pool filled with saltwater. Finally, they're returned to their ocean homes.

This is card number

Doctors there have also treated turtles with a mysterious virus. The virus made these turtles too weak to lift their heads. Doctors fed the turtles special squid shakes to help them get strong again.

This is card number

Terrific Titles

Materials

● nonfiction books, magazines, and newspapers

WRITING SKILLS Students will learn to write effective titles that summarize the focus of their reports and catch readers' attention.

Titles With Words That Rhyme

How to Be Heart Smart

Titles With Words That Start With the Same Letter (*Alliteration*)

Weird Winter Weather

Titles That Paint Pictures or Make Comparisons

Rain Forests: Nature's Green Umbrella

Titles With Plays on Words

What's the Buzz About Bees?

Titles That Tell Exactly What Is in the Report

Five Ways Kids Can Help the Earth

What draws your attention to a particular article in a magazine or newspaper? Chances are, it's a well-written headline or title. Titles serve two main purposes: (1) to let the reader know the gist of the report or story, and (2) to grab the reader's attention so that he or she wants to keep reading. In this activity students review different kinds of titles and practice writing effective titles for their own reports.

Prewriting

◎ Have each student cut out or copy one nonfiction title they think works well. It may be the title of a book or book chapter, the headline of a newspaper or magazine article, or even the title of a pamphlet or brochure. (This works well as a homework assignment.) Invite each student to explain why that particular title caught his or her attention.

◎ Place each of the titles in the appropriate category. Display them in a scrapbook or on a bulletin board. The list at left includes some categories to start with.

Writing and Revising

1 Have students write a working title for their reports early on in the writing process (at the start of the drafting phase or even earlier). This title need not be perfect; its primary purpose is to remind the writer of the focus of the report (for example, "How Dogs Help People").

2 Once students have finished writing their drafts, they should revise their titles, keeping in mind that they need to grab their audience's attention. Provide access to the Terrific Titles collection you compiled during the prewriting stage. Encourage students to try writing several types of titles before settling on a favorite.

Editing and Publishing

Have students work in pairs to make sure their titles match their reports. Point out that it's better to have a simple title that makes sense than a rhyming title that misleads the reader.

Add Spice to Sentences

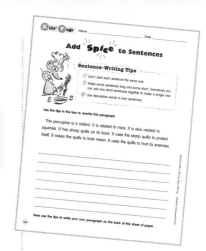

WRITING SKILLS Students will learn to vary sentence length and construction.

One of the most common pitfalls of young students' writing is the tendency to start every sentence the same way and to make every sentence about the same length. Before long, the poor reader is on snooze control! Teach students to make their sentences more interesting by starting with different words and using both short and long sentences.

Prewriting

◎ Read aloud the two paragraphs below right, or copy them onto chart paper for everyone to see. Ask students to describe the differences between the two pieces. Ask: "Which paragraph sounds more interesting? Why?" List students' responses on the board.

Writing and Revising

1 Distribute the Add Spice to Sentences reproducible on page 46 and review the sentence-writing tips at the top of the page. Explain that students will rewrite the paragraph using these tips. Remind students that they can use their own words.

2 Once students have finished the rewriting exercise, ask a few volunteers to read aloud their new paragraphs. Note how each student has created an original paragraph, and point out any sentences that are particularly well-written.

3 Now ask students to apply the sentence-writing tips to their own reports. On the back of the reproducible, students can write one or more paragraphs on their own topics, making sure to start sentences in different ways, write sentences of varying lengths, and use a variety of descriptive words.

Editing and Publishing

Have students edit their work using the checklist on page 54. Keep in mind that, in their enthusiasm, some students may have combined too many sentences and created run-ons. Help students edit to make sure each sentence has a subject and verb and is clear and easy to understand.

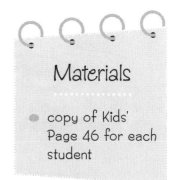

Materials

● copy of Kids' Page 46 for each student

Paragraph 1

Ben Franklin was a great inventor. He was born in 1847. He was born in Ohio. He was not good in school. He grew up to be an inventor. He invented many great things. He invented electric lights and the phonograph.

Paragraph 2

Ben Franklin was one of our country's greatest inventors. He was born in Ohio in 1847. As a child, Franklin did not do well in school. But when he grew up, he was a big success. He invented many useful things, such as electric lights and the phonograph.

Add Spice to Sentences

Sentence-Writing Tips

◎ Don't start each sentence the same way.

◎ Make some sentences long and some short. Sometimes you can join two short sentences together to make a longer one.

◎ Use descriptive words in your sentences.

Use the tips in the box to rewrite this paragraph.

The porcupine is a rodent. It is related to mice. It is also related to squirrels. It has sharp quills on its back. It uses the sharp quills to protect itself. It raises the quills to look mean. It uses the quills to hurt its enemies.

_____

_____

_____

_____

_____

_____

Now use the tips to write your own paragraph on the back of this sheet of paper.

Building Skills in Writing: Report Writing   Scholastic Professional Books

Question-and-Answer Peekaboo Book

WRITING SKILLS Students will learn about presentation by using this creative report format.

As teachers, your challenge is not simply to teach your second- or third-graders to write; it is to help them learn to *enjoy* writing. That's easy to do when you provide creative report formats for students to use. Students will have so much fun putting these question-and-answer mini-books together, they'll forget that report-writing is supposed to be hard work! An added advantage of writing in Q & A format is that focusing on specific questions helps young writers identify and stick to main ideas.

Prewriting

◎ Have students thoroughly research their topics. For best results, have them use the All the Answers grid on page 31 to identify research questions and take notes. This will help students organize their reports in a question-and-answer format.

Writing and Revising

1 Have students write early drafts of their questions and answers on plain paper. Each answer should be one or two paragraphs long. When students are happy with the drafts, they can copy their work onto the peekaboo book template.

2 Direct students to cut out the pattern along the outer dotted lines and then again along the center horizontal dotted line, creating two rectangular strips. Each of these strips is one page of the mini-book. Provide as many copies as students need.

Materials

- copies of Kids' Page 49 (two or more copies per student, depending on how many questions they would like to answer)
- construction paper
- scissors
- markers or crayons
- stapler

3 Tell students to write their questions on the lines at the far left of each strip. Have them write the answers to these questions on the lines at the right.

4 Then have students fold the right side of each strip in to meet the vertical solid line, covering the answer.

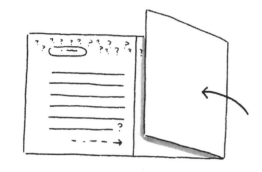

5 Students can use the blank parts of the folded strips to draw maps, illustrations, diagrams, and other visual aids related to their questions.

6 Compile the peekaboo books by stacking the pages and stapling the left edge. Students can create colorful covers for their mini-books by tracing the page onto construction paper and cutting it out. On the cover, have kids write a catchy report title (see page 44) and their names. To read the mini-books, simply lift the peekaboo flap after each question.

Editing and Publishing

After students have checked for spelling and grammar mistakes, display the peekaboo books in your classroom library or reading corner. Encourage students to borrow one another's books at independent reading time.

Answer

Answer

Question

Lift to find out

Question

Lift to find out

Materials

- access to computers with word-processing programs

Create a Classroom Magazine

WRITING SKILLS Students will synthesize all of the writing skills introduced in this book, from selecting a topic to editing and publishing.

Students love to feel like published authors! By compiling student reports into a magazine, every writer in your class gets to see his or her name in print. This activity works best when students have written reports based on a common theme, giving a focus to your magazine. Individual student subtopics will provide the angles for your articles.

Prewriting

- Bring in children's magazines for students to read (see page 10). Identify and discuss the major elements of a magazine article: headline, byline (writer's name), article, photos, photo captions, maps, and other graphics.

- Select your common theme based on a topic you're currently studying or on a subject students would like to know more about. Then have students select individual subtopics and conduct research.

Writing and Revising

Use the other lessons in this chapter to introduce or review specific drafting skills and techniques: writing paragraphs, focusing on main ideas, varying sentence construction, putting ideas in order, writing titles, and so on. Have students use these skills to write rough drafts of their articles on the computer. Then have them use the Editing My Report checklist on page 54 to make sure they've satisfied the criteria for an effective report.

Editing and Publishing

- Pair up students for peer editing. Students can help each another find and fix mistakes in spelling, punctuation, and capitalization.

- After you've double-checked each article, use a word-processing program to help students design the layout of each page (one article per page). Make headlines larger and bolder than the body of the article and type students' names beneath them. Provide space where students can put maps, charts, or illustrations.

- Make a cover for the magazine, featuring its title (students can make suggestions, then vote for a favorite) as well as "teasers" or short blurbs for a few of the articles inside. The cover should also have an illustration or photo that reflects the theme of the magazine. Distribute the magazine to students, parents, and faculty.

Other Creative Report Formats

Looking for an inventive way for students to present their reports? Try one of these exciting ideas!

Top-Five Lists

Invite students to organize their reports numerically, with a paragraph for each subtopic. Examples include: The Top Five Reasons to Exercise, Five Things Kids Can Do to Prevent Fires, or The Top Three Endangered Animals.

Cereal-Box Reports

Turn an empty cereal box into an informative, three-dimensional report. First, cut off the top of the box and glue construction paper onto the four sides of the box. Have students glue the first page of their report onto one of the larger sides of the box. On the reverse side, glue the continuation of the report and/or supporting diagrams, illustrations, maps, or graphs. On the two narrow sides of the box, students can list the sources they used or provide additional fun facts about their topics. Make the boxes even more fun by having each writer put an "artifact" inside his or her box. Artifacts can be anything that adds information to the report. For example, a student reporting on autumn might put a few colorful leaves in the box. A student writing about France might include a miniature flag or a souvenir from a recent trip there. Students can attach an index-card label to each artifact.

Postcard Reports

When students are writing reports on places (such as animal habitats, our national parks, or countries of the world), use large index cards to make your own postcards. Students can write their reports on a series of four or five postcards, using one side for text and the other side for relevant illustrations. For example, a student writing about Yosemite National Park might write four postcards: one to introduce the park; one about Old Faithful, the park's most famous geyser; one about moose and other animals that live in the park; and one about the wildfires that have affected the park. When launching this type of project, it's a good idea to bring in some examples of postcards so that students become familiar with the format.

Reports in Rhyme

More experienced writers may want to try writing their reports as poems or raps. They can then perform their reports for the whole class.

Wrapping Up Reports: Suggestions for Editing, Publishing, and Assessing

Many specific tips for editing, publishing, and assessing students' reports are found in the preceding chapters. The following are some additional general suggestions, checklists, and rubrics to assist you and your students in the final stages of the report-writing process.

Editing

Consider having students pair up to edit each other's reports. This technique, called peer editing, is a great way to give students confidence and inspire cooperation. (Of course, you should have a final look at a report before the writer moves on to the final draft.) Distribute copies of the Editing My Report checklist on page 54 for students to use as they edit their own and each other's reports. Student writers should hand in a copy of this checklist along with their final projects to show that they have completed the self-editing and peer-editing processes.

To streamline the editing process, provide students with a copy of the Editing Symbols checklist on page 55.

Publishing

As I mentioned in chapter 3, a creative format can help motivate young report writers. Use one of the concepts described in that section, or come up with your own. You can often brainstorm fabulous publishing ideas directly related to the topics students are researching. For example, if students are writing reports on nutrition, you might compile reports and favorite recipes in a classroom cookbook and then sell copies of the cookbook to members of the school community as a charity fundraiser. One teacher I know had students write reports on insects. Her publishing idea? Students made Old-West-style "Wanted" posters for the bugs they researched.

Since the crux of publishing is actually having one's work read by others, go all-out to create opportunities for students to share their reports. Plan a "Let's Discover" morning in your classroom, and invite other classes to come in and look at students' reports. If your school has a Web site, look into creating a page for students' current reports. By participating in putting their work online, students will learn valuable computer skills. And parents will relish being able to show off their child's work to faraway family members!

Assessment

Don't make your assessment criteria a big mystery! Before students begin a writing project, let them know what you're looking for by providing an easy-to-understand checklist (see, for example, the one on page 54). You can tailor this or any checklist to the demands of your specific project.

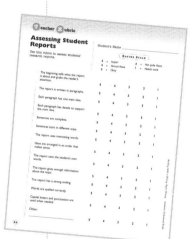

When the time comes to evaluate how well students have met your criteria, use a rubric. A rubric goes beyond recording whether or not a certain component is present; it actually provides a scale that allows you to assign a score to each facet of a student's work. On page 56, you'll find a rubric designed to help you assess both content and mechanics in nearly any report-writing project. You may copy and use the rubric as is or adapt it to suit your individual needs. You can also provide copies to students so that they can evaluate their own reports. By conferencing with students and discussing their self- evaluations, you can get a good handle on students' level of skill and comfort with the writing process.

As with any type of writing, have students keep portfolios of their writing to show progress over time. You can create folders specifically for reports, or combine all of your students' writing projects in a single portfolio. Parents will enjoy browsing through their child's report-writing portfolio at conference time, and you'll have an ongoing testament to each student's progress.

Name _____ Date _____

Editing My Report

Before you hand in your report, work with a partner to make sure it is in tip-top shape. Put a ✔ next to each item after you check it. Ask your partner to do the same.

	I checked.	Partner checked.
The title and the beginning of the report grab the reader's attention.	◯	◯
The report is organized into paragraphs in an order that makes sense.	◯	◯
Each paragraph has a main idea.	◯	◯
Each paragraph has sentences that support the main idea.	◯	◯
All of the information in the report belongs.	◯	◯
The sentences don't all begin the same way.	◯	◯
There are long and short sentences.	◯	◯
The report uses interesting, descriptive words.	◯	◯
Paragraphs are indented.	◯	◯
The sentences end in periods, question marks, or exclamation points.	◯	◯
Commas are used when needed. Other punctuation is used correctly.	◯	◯

Building Skills in Writing: Report Writing

Scholastic Professional Books

Name _____ Date _____

Editing Symbols

Use these symbols when you edit your own writing and your classmates' writing.

Symbol	It Means	Example
≡	Use a capital letter.	Atlanta, georgia ‗
/	Use a lowercase letter.	I like chocolate ℓake.
∧	Insert (add) something.	*my* Colin is brother. ∧
ℓ	Remove something.	It is ~~very~~ very hot.
⊙	Add a period.	The rain fell ⊙
⋏	Add a comma.	I have dogs cats, and fish. ⋏
¶	Indent for a new paragraph.	¶ Later that day, Marcie heard a noise.
∼	Transpose (switch position).	Th(ie)r house is nearby.

Assessing Student Reports

Use this rubric to assess students'
research reports.

Student's Name _____

5 = Super! 2 = Not quite there
4 = Almost there 1 = Needs work
3 = Okay

The beginning tells what the report is about and grabs the reader's attention. 5	4	3	2	I

Statement	5	4	3	2	1
The beginning tells what the report is about and grabs the reader's attention.	5	4	3	2	I
The report is written in paragraphs.	5	4	3	2	I
Each paragraph has one main idea.	5	4	3	2	I
Each paragraph has details to support the main idea.	5	4	3	2	I
Sentences are complete.	5	4	3	2	I
Sentences start in different ways.	5	4	3	2	I
The report uses interesting words.	5	4	3	2	I
Ideas are arranged in an order that makes sense.	5	4	3	2	I
The report uses the student's own words.	5	4	3	2	I
The report gives enough information about the topic.	5	4	3	2	I
The report has a strong ending.	5	4	3	2	I
Words are spelled correctly.	5	4	3	2	I
Capital letters and punctuation are used when needed.	5	4	3	2	I
Other: _____	5	4	3	2	I

Building Skills in Writing: Report Writing Scholastic Professional Books